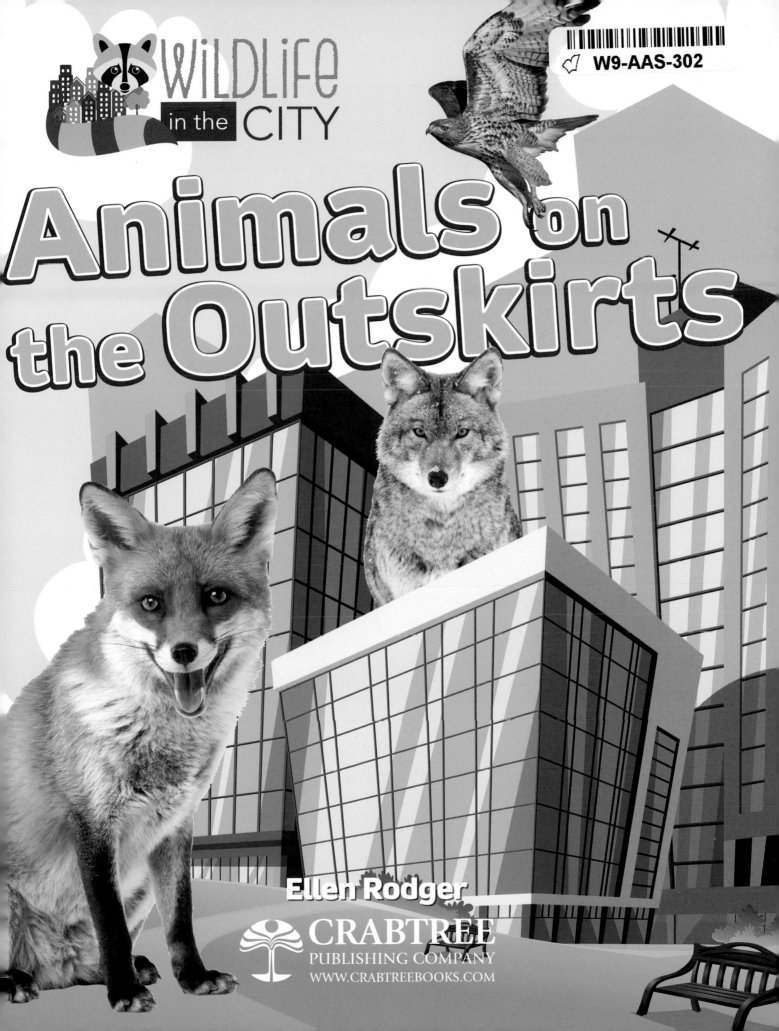

Wildlife
in the CITY

Animals on the Outskirts

Ellen Rodger

CRABTREE
PUBLISHING COMPANY
WWW.CRABTREEBOOKS.COM

Author: Ellen Rodger

Editorial director: Kathy Middleton

Art director: Rosie Gowsell Pattison

Editor: Petrice Custance

Proofreader: Wendy Scavuzzo

**Production coordinator and
  Prepress technician:** Ken Wright

Print coordinator: Katherine Berti

Images

All images from Shutterstock

Produced for Crabtree Publishing by

Plan B Book Packagers

www.planbbookpackagers.com

Library and Archives Canada Cataloguing in Publication

Title: Animals on the outskirts / Ellen Rodger.
Names: Rodger, Ellen, author.
Description: Series statement: Wildlife in the city | Includes index.
Identifiers: Canadiana (print) 20190128305 |
  Canadiana (ebook) 20190128313 |
  ISBN 9780778766872 (hardcover) |
  ISBN 9780778766971 (softcover) |
  ISBN 9781427124142 (HTML)
Subjects: LCSH: Urban animals—Juvenile literature. | LCSH: Wildlife
  pests—Juvenile literature. | LCSH: Urban ecology (Sociology)—Juvenile
  literature. | LCSH: Human-animal relationships. | LCSH: Nature—Effect of
  human beings on—Juvenile literature.
Classification: LCC QH541.5.C6 R63 2019 | DDC j591.75/6—dc23

Library of Congress Cataloging-in-Publication Data

CIP available at the Library of Congress

LCCN: 2019025176

Crabtree Publishing Company
www.crabtreebooks.com   1-800-387-7650

Printed in the U.S.A./102019/CG20190809

Published in Canada
Crabtree Publishing
616 Welland Ave.
St. Catharines, Ontario
L2M 5V6

Published in the United States
Crabtree Publishing
PMB 59051
350 Fifth Avenue, 59th Floor
New York, New York 10118

Published in the United Kingdom
Crabtree Publishing
Maritime House
Basin Road North, Hove
BN41 1WR

Published in Australia
Crabtree Publishing
Unit 3–5 Currumbin Court
Capalaba
QLD 4157

CONTENTS

WILD IN YOUR NEIGHBORHOOD

A home in the **suburbs** used to mean a quiet life. But as cities grow and sprawl outward, the areas outside the **core** are becoming wilder. Wilder with animals, that is. Yards and parks in suburbs are quiet homes for **urban** wild animals. They offer a **smorgasbord** of greens and garbage for deer, red foxes, coyotes, cardinals, and more.

Urban or suburban sprawl is the expansion of cities and towns into surrounding land. When we build homes in animal territory, we are bound to see animals in our backyards.

SURVIVORS ON THE FRINGE

These wild animals are what **biologists** call human **adapters**. As we make our homes near their homes, these once-shy creatures become bolder. They change to fit the conditions around them. They alter the way they forage, or find food, and where they have their babies. In suburban areas, plant-eating animals find tasty meals in green gardens. **Predators** track down **prey** on golf courses and green spaces. Adapters do not need humans. They will survive with or without us. The question is, can we live peacefully with them?

There is a lot of disagreement among humans about coyotes. Some people love them, while others want these wild canines out of suburban areas.

Urban Coyote Research Project

Want to get up close and personal with a coyote? Head to Illinois! Based in Chicago, the Urban Coyote Research Program allows scientists to learn more about city-dwelling coyotes, and how we can **coexist** with them. They do this by safely capturing coyotes, putting a special collar on them, and tracking where they go. The coyotes are watched to understand how they live in and around cities. The tracking studies show that humans and coyotes coexist mostly without problems. Most coyotes were shown to be helpful to suburban **ecosystems**. They prey on rats, Canada geese, and deer, and keep these animals from overrunning suburban areas.

HOME HABITAT

Areas on the fringe of cities and urban woodlands are a land of plenty for urban wild animals. Plenty of food and **habitat**, that is!

Urban white-tailed deer make their homes in forested areas. They feed on leafy grasses, mushrooms, berries, acorns, and garden plants.

Cardinal populations have increased in suburban areas where they can find more of their favorite foods, such as sunflower seeds. They nest in backyards, bushes, and along forest edges.

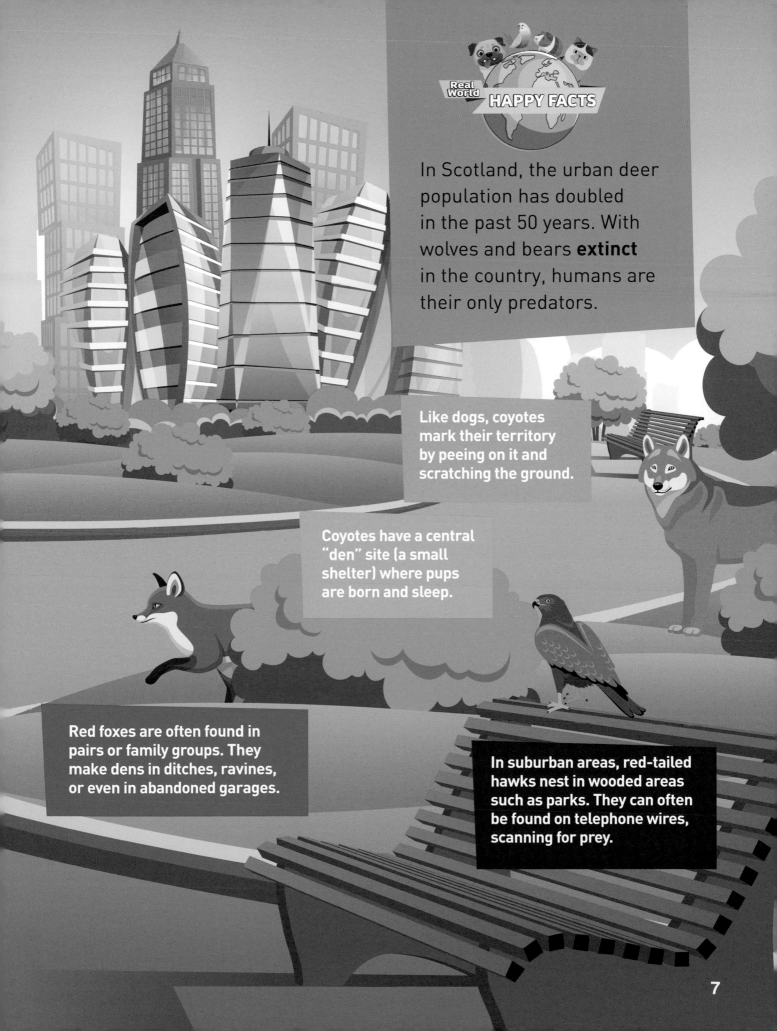

Real World HAPPY FACTS

In Scotland, the urban deer population has doubled in the past 50 years. With wolves and bears **extinct** in the country, humans are their only predators.

Like dogs, coyotes mark their territory by peeing on it and scratching the ground.

Coyotes have a central "den" site (a small shelter) where pups are born and sleep.

Red foxes are often found in pairs or family groups. They make dens in ditches, ravines, or even in abandoned garages.

In suburban areas, red-tailed hawks nest in wooded areas such as parks. They can often be found on telephone wires, scanning for prey.

ECO-THERMOMETERS

Adapter animals are sometimes called "eco-thermometers." It means that in urban environments, animal adapters give us hints about the changing environment. Like a thermometer, their presence and strength in urban and suburban areas reflects the temperature, or health of the ecosystem. When they are healthy, the city ecosystem is healthy. Adapters both hunt and **scavenge** for food. Some even evolve to suit their landscape. This means they gradually change their bodies and habits to better fit into the neighborhood.

Deer eating your garden? Some people put up electrified fences to keep them away. Covering plants with wire cages is less cruel.

NEW WAYS

Anole lizards are native to Caribbean forests, where they run on tree branches. In urban areas, this lizard runs along the slippery tiles and straight walls of houses. Anoles have developed an unusual adaptation to make this easier: their legs have become longer and their feet stickier. City anoles have evolved with more lamellae, or fine hair-like plates, on the underside of their toes. This helps them grip smooth human-made surfaces such as walls, tiles, and windows. Anoles feast on insects, making them a welcome house guest. Some adapters aren't as well liked. Homeowners use baited traps and sometimes poisons to rid their backyards of suburban wildlife they see as pests.

Urban Biodiversity Monitoring

The Urban Wildlife Information Network (UWIN) is the world's largest wildlife monitoring network. UWIN studies the **biodiversity** of animals that live in urban areas and tries to find solutions to human–wildlife conflicts. UWIN encourages **citizen scientists** to watch and report on the wildlife in their neighborhoods. This helps people realize where and how animals live. The 12-member network was started by the Lincoln Park Zoo in Chicago. It now includes the U.S. National Parks Service, San Francisco Parks Department, zoos, and universities. They install cameras in parks, cemeteries, and forest preserves to take photos. Deer are the number-one species spotted by all network members. A moose caught on camera in Edmonton, Alberta in Canada was the largest animal spotted.

UWIN cameras help researchers study the behavior of animals. One goal is to build greener cities with strong ecosystems.

FOX IN THE GARDEN!

In many areas of the world, fox populations are higher in cities and suburbs than in **rural** areas. Foxes do well with the good food supplies in these areas. In most cases, they are better fed than their country cousins. One reason for this is people feeding them scraps and pet food.

Foxes seek out ecotones. Ecotones are areas of land that transition with different types of vegetation, such as from grassland to forest.

Foxes use sheds and barns as shelters. In some areas, they even make dens under porches.

FOXY BEHAVIOR

Foxes are a great example of synanthropes. These are animals that live near or around humans and benefit from human neighbors. They are often considered a nuisance. For example, is your garden always dug up? Are chickens disappearing from your urban coop? You might look to a synanthrope as the culprit. In the United Kingdom, foxes are found in every town and city. At the same time, the rural fox population has declined 34 percent in the last 20 years. Much of that is because farmers view them as pests that prey on farm animals such as chickens. Urban foxes are not usually hunted. They are also less fearful of other animals, including coyotes. In urban areas, biologists have noticed that these natural enemies appear to coexist.

Canid Projects

Have you seen a fox in your neighborhood? Well, if you live in Madison, Wisconsin you can report your sighting or volunteer to help researchers there map the locations of these animals. The Urban Canid Project studies foxes and coyotes. Canids are members of the dog family. Researchers from the University of Wisconsin-Madison live trap foxes and coyotes in the city and fit them with radio collars. Their aim is to learn more about how the animals live in the city and get along with humans. It's not the only group that studies urban foxes. The Canid Project is a charity that educates people about **conservation** through wildlife photography and animal rescues.

FANTASTIC FOX

Much like their wilderness cousins, wolves, foxes are often portrayed as **cunning** tricksters because of their ability to escape hunters. In urban areas, foxes like to keep to themselves.

Not all red foxes are red! Some can be silver-y, black, or brown, and sometimes you might get all the colors in one litter of pups!

In urban and suburban areas, foxes have smaller territories of about 1.2 to 1.8 square miles (3 to 4.6 sq km). This can include a leafy section of a park or backyard. They have been known to use sheds for shelter.

Red foxes breed from mid-January to late February. Fox litters can be as large as 11 pups (also called cubs). Pups are born blind and don't open their eyes until nine days after birth.

Urban foxes appear not to fear humans. They have learned that humans are slow-moving animals. With an average running speed of 30 miles per hour (48 kph), foxes can easily outrun a human if threatened.

You might spot a fox in your neighborhood at night. They prefer hunting when it is dark and use their cat-like eyesight to spot prey.

Foxes are omnivores, meaning they will eat plants as well as animals such as birds, rabbits, small reptiles, and insects. They may dig through garbage in urban areas.

COYOTES AND COYWOLVES

Coyotes are small- to medium-sized animal adapters that are often mistaken for **domesticated** dogs. They look that similar! When you look more closely, coyotes have a distinct, narrow face, pointed ears, and mottled coloring. This certainly isn't Fido!

If you see a coyote in your yard, it is likely because there is food or shelter there. Keep your trash locked up until garbage day. Don't keep pet food outside, and pick up fruit that has fallen from trees.

LIVING WELL

Coyotes are survivors. They can be found living in all sorts of habitats where there is a food source, from forests to backyards. Another example of the coyote's adaptability is coywolves. Coywolves are hybrids of western coyotes and eastern wolves. They have expanded their territory over the past 100 years. This hybrid is a result of threats to each species, including cutting down forests and hunting. Some scientists insist that "coywolves" are eastern coyotes. They are a mix of coyote, wolf, and dog and are a result of years of interbreeding.

Coyote print   *Dog print*

Look Around You

We don't need to see an animal with our eyes to prove that we share a home or backyard with them. Animals leave clues that we can spot if we know where and how to look for them. Urban coyotes have altered their behavior to better avoid humans. Instead of hunting at dawn and dusk, they roam during the day. Keep an eye or ear out for these members of the canine family and write down coyote signs in a notebook. Watch for tracks in mud. Coyote prints are larger than dog paw prints. The biggest differences are that coyote tracks tend to be farther apart than dogs, due to a longer stride. Tracks will most often be in a straighter line. Their scat, or poop, will usually contain hair and small bones.

COYOTE CALLING

Coyotes are ecosystem balancers. They are territorial and keep other coyotes out of their territory. They also prey on other animals in their territories and help ensure that the ecosystem isn't overrun by rodents or deer.

Dens are well hidden, often in unlikely places such as drainage tunnels and golf courses.

A coyote's diet can expand thanks to the humans around them. It can grow to include food waste (garbage), small outdoor pets, and livestock such as chickens.

Coyote territory may include golf courses and soccer fields.

They are apex predators, or the top predator in an ecosystem.

Being coyote-aware helps you and urban coyotes. Most coyotes are easily scared by humans. If you encounter one, you can scare them off by raising your arms in the air and stomping your feet. This is called hazing.

They avoid residential areas, but may be seen occasionally strolling down a street within their territory.

Coyotes help slow the growth of suburban deer populations by preying on fawns.

Males help feed and raise pups.

OH DEER!

In many suburban areas, deer populations are exploding. In the U.K., the deer population is the highest it has been for 1,000 years. That means a lot of deer munching their way through gardens and bushes.

Males have antlers that regrow each year. Very few females have antlers.

Deer are very active at dusk and at night which can make driving in deer territory tricky.

Their preferred foods include leaves, woody plants, grass, herbs, mushrooms, and even blueberries! They also eat garden plants and flowers as well as farm crops such as corn.

White-tailed deer eat a lot. In more urban areas, you might see deer grazing on grass at the side of the road, in your garden, or wandering through your backyard.

White tailed deer earned their name because of the white fur on the underside of their tails and on their behinds!

Deer mate in the fall. Fawns are born in late spring. Female deer hide their fawns for the first few weeks after they are born.

In areas where there are not many animals preying on deer, their populations grow quickly.

Real World HAPPY FACTS

Some North American cities have urban deer management plans. These plans use **repellants** to keep deer away from gardens, as well as fencing and landscaping that keep deer away. When deer are killed, the meat must be donated to charity.

WILD CATS

When you think of wild cats, what comes to mind? Maybe a lion **stealthily** searching for food in Botswana, or a tiger lazily sleeping in the sun in Nepal? Well, look no farther than your own backyard to get a glimpse of North America's wild cats! These animals, although smaller than their large-maned or orange-striped relatives, are incredibly adaptable.

Cats prefer to stay hidden. This helps them be better hunters.

SURVIVING FIRES AND DROUGHTS

Cougars, or mountain lions, are becoming increasingly common in cities in the southwestern United States. Their traditional territory in Nevada, California, Utah, and Arizona is becoming hotter and drier due to **climate change**. The dryness forces their prey to greener pastures. It also leads to more forest fires. Cougar territory is also more broken up. This means more humans are building homes and businesses where they live, forcing them to cross into human settlements as they move about hunting or looking for mates. Experts believe even more big cats will move closer to green suburbs and farm lands in the future.

Studies show that Mumbai's leopards actually help people by preying on the estimated 100,000 stray dogs in the city. This reduces the risk of rabies, a disease spread by dog bites and scratches that is costly to treat.

Cat-Human Tensions

Imagine living in a city where leopards roam the streets! Mumbai, India is home to 20 million people and about 35 leopards. The spotted big cats are protected in a large urban forest called Sanjay Gandhi National Park. The city grew up around the leopard territory, and now millions of people live on the fringe of this leopard habitat. The cats enter the city at night looking for food. They are attracted by garbage dumped on the edge of the park, but they also eat stray dogs, rodents, and wild boars.

BOBCAT IN THE BACKYARD

Bobcats look like the biggest house cats you have ever seen. They are double the size of domesticated cats but still small in wild cat terms. These forest and **brushland** animals have adapted to life on the fringes of urban areas.

Bobcats mark their territories with poop, scent, and by scraping trees.

They have territories, or home ranges, of 3.2 square miles (8.3 square km) for males and 1.5 square miles (3.9 square km) for females. Ranges are smaller when there are more bobcats in the area.

Urban bobcats live in parks surrounded by urban development throughout the U.S., Canada, and Mexico. They are becoming more comfortable around humans.

Bobcats can jump fences of more than 6 feet (1.8 m) high. Homeowners attach woven or hot wire to the top of their fences to keep them out.

Strict limits on hunting may be behind the growing number of bobcats in urban areas. Bobcats were hunted for **bounties** in many states until the late 1970s when new laws were passed to protect them. Today, they are a conservation success story, with populations steady and growing.

Litters of two to four kittens are born between February and June in areas such as California. Northern bobcats may have their litters a little later in the year. Kits may be born in quiet places such as hollowed logs or drain tunnels.

Bobcats are prey animals that hunt at night. They eat rabbits, gophers, squirrels, and woodrats, but will also eat seeds and nuts from backyard bird feeders.

FLIGHTS OF FANCY

Look up! Way up! Animal adapters don't just live in the grass or under the ground. We can find lots of them living in the trees! These birds have learned to thrive in changing environments due to urban development. For example, in Barbados, a study was done that determined urban bullfinches were much less skittish around humans than their rural relatives. Some even snatched food from humans!

CHANGED BY THE CITY

European blackbirds used to be forest birds until they started moving to cities a few hundred years ago. They have been urban birds for so long now that the species has adapted and physically changed. City blackbirds have shorter beaks than their country cousins. They also don't migrate, they breed earlier, and they sing differently. In fact, researchers think the blackbird's higher-pitched song in the city may be a response to noise from traffic and construction. The birds are evolving to suit their environment.

In cities, hawks like to position themselves on high branches of trees or on light and utility posts. This allows them to scan for prey—other birds and rodents.

> *Cities are increasingly important habitats for raptors. There is plenty of prey, including pigeons and doves.*

Look Around You

Urban raptors—no these aren't dinosaurs, or a basketball team—are another name for birds of prey found in urban areas. These owls, eagles, vultures, and hawks are especially good at adapting to their changing habitat. Finding some in your neighborhood should not be difficult. First, you need to know what each raptor looks like. Raptors have large wingspans and sharp, hooked claws called talons. HawkWatch International is a conservation group that helps protect these regal raptors and educate people about them. HawkWatch conducts watches to track migrating raptors in North America. Go to their website at hawkwatch.org to find a HawkWatch site and information on identifying raptors in your area.

URBAN HAWK

Red-tailed hawks are birds of prey sometimes called chickenhawks in the United States. They have a wide range in North America—from the northern tips of the Canadian provinces to southern Mexico and Central America.

City hawks are not hard to spot. They often perch on poles or roofs in order to scan for prey below them

The red-tailed hawk is the most common type of hawk found in North America. They use their talons to capture prey and eat rodents, other birds, squirrels, and reptiles.

Red-tailed hawks nest in trees and ledges of buildings. Nests are made from leaves and branches with softer material on the inside. They lay from 2 to 4 eggs and incubate them for 28 to 35 days.

Researchers from the University of Wisconsin have found that red-tailed hawks help city residents connect with nature. In a 2017 study, they interviewed people and found that most viewed hawks positively. Researchers believe this view can translate into an interest in conserving the environment for hawks.

Males and females work together to raise chicks. Chicks can fly and leave the nest at about 6 to 7 weeks.

They have a whitish underbelly and brownish-red head and body.

These hawks are efficient hunters. They prefer wide-open areas to hunt and like to perch on tall trees or even telephone poles in the city. There, they have a better view to spot all of the tasty mice, squirrels, rabbits, and reptiles.

ANIMAL ADAPTERS AROUND THE WORLD

Wild animals have always lived in cities. In ancient Egypt, wealthy people kept baboons and hippos as pets. Leopards and crocodiles were known to venture into Egyptian cities as well—looking for meals. Humans have built cities and homes in almost every animal habitat.

Conservation group Baboon Matters Trust believes teaching people not to feed baboons and how to baboon-proof gardens and garbage is better than culling, or reducing the population by hunting some.

BABOON VANDALS?

Chacma baboon territory is spread throughout a variety of habitats in southern Africa. In Cape Town, South Africa, these large monkeys have been known to raid houses and restaurants for food. To curb their raiding behavior, the city began clamping down on baboons. Male baboons who lead raiding groups were culled. Critics say killing the baboons does not eliminate the problem. They feel less drastic plans such as educating people on how to live with the baboons is better for both animals and people.

Urban areas are warmer than surrounding countryside because of concrete buildings and paved roads. Dragon Project researchers say this has forced water dragons to bury their eggs deeper in urban areas.

The Dragon Project

The eastern water dragon is an Australian lizard that is shy in the wild but less so in cities. The Dragon Project is studying more than 650 of the lizards in the city of Brisbane. Researchers want to see how they have adjusted to living around humans. It is the largest urban wildlife monitoring project in Australia. The dragons live in parks near water. Researchers believe people should watch and listen to urban animals to learn how they communicate with us. The dragons nod their heads, slap their tails, and wave their arms to tell humans when to stay clear of their territory. When humans understand them, there is less conflict.

LEARNING MORE

Books

Carney, Elizabeth. *Everything Big Cats.* National Geographic Kids, 2011.

Hansen, Grace. *Coyotes.* Abdo Publishing, 2016.

Hoena, Blake. *Everything Birds of Prey.* National Geographic Kids, 2015.

Kalman, Bobbie. *What is a Top Predator?* Crabtree Publishing, 2012.

Spelman, Lucy. *National Geographic Animal Encyclopedia.* National Geographic, 2012.

Websites

www.humanesociety.org/resources/coyote-hazing
The U.S. Humane Society has tips on how to discourage coyotes from visiting your neighborhood.

https://urbancoyoteresearch.com/about-project
This website has information on the Urban Coyote Research Program as well as on coyotes in general and how to avoid conflicts with coyotes in urban areas.

http://baboonmatters.org.za
Baboon Matters is a conservation organization that helps create awareness of human–baboon conflicts. Their website has cool news and stories on their work and understanding baboons.

GLOSSARY

adapters Living things that change or become used to new conditions

biodiversity A variety of life in a particular habitat

biologists Scientists who study living things such as plants and animals and their environments

bounties Money paid for killing or capturing an animal

brushland Wild lands that are not farmed and where wild animals roam

canines Animals related to dogs or the dog family of animals

citizen scientists Ordinary people who do scientific work such as counting the number of birds in a forest on a given day

climate change A change in global or regional climate patterns caused by increased levels of carbon dioxide in Earth's atmosphere

coexist Live peacefully in the same place

conservation The act of preserving and protecting wildlife

core The center of something, such as a town

culling Reducing the population of a wild animal through selective hunting or killing

cunning Showing skill in getting what is desired by being sly

development Converting land to a new purpose by constructing buildings or using its resources

domesticated Describing animals that are tame or live closely with humans

ecosystems Communities in nature where different living things exist together or interact

extinct When all members of a species have died

habitat The natural environment of a living thing, or the place where they are usually found living

predators Animals that kill and eat other animals

prey Animals that are hunted and killed by other animals for food

repellents Something that causes disgust to deter animals from approaching

rural Of or from the countryside

scavenge To search through and collect discarded waste for food

smorgasbord A buffet of hot and cold foods where people serve themselves

stealthily Cautiously, without being seen or heard

suburbs An area where people live outside of a city or large town

urban Of or relating to a town or city

INDEX

QUESTIONS & ANSWERS

Q: What should I do if I find an injured hawk or deer in my backyard?

A: The best thing to do is phone the local Humane Society, animal control, or wildlife rescue. If you can't find one, a local veterinarian or government office might be able to help.

Q: Is it true that if you trap and kill coyotes you can get rid of them in your neighborhood?

A: Trapping and killing is one method used by some cities to rid areas of problem coyotes. However, coyotes removed from one area will be replaced by others. When their population is controlled by culls, they have more babies and at an earlier age.